# Foundations of Christian Doctrine
## Self Study Guide

# Kevin J. Conner

Original Edition
© Copyright 1998 Kevin J. Conner

This Edition
© Copyright 2026 Conner Ministries Ltd

It is illegal and a violation of Christian ethics to reproduce any or parts or diagrams in this book without written permission of the author or publishers.

CONNER
MINISTRIES

Published by Conner Ministries Ltd

WEB: kevinconner.org
Email: admin@kevinconner.org

## About the Author

Born in Melbourne, Australia in 1927 and saved at the age of 14, Kevin Conner served the Lord in the Salvation Army until the age of 21. At this time he entered pastoral ministry for several years. After that, he was involved in teaching ministry in Australia, New Zealand and for many years at Bible Temple in Portland, Oregon. After serving as Senior Minister of Waverley Christian Fellowship for eight years (1987-1994), he continued to serve the church locally as well as ministering at various conferences and the continued writing of textbooks.

Kevin was recognized internationally as a teaching-apostle after his many years in both church and Bible College ministry. His textbooks have been used by ministers and students throughout the world. He was in great demand as a teacher and has travelled extensively. Kevin passed away peacefully in Melbourne, Australia in February 2019 at the age of 92.

Visit Kevin's web site at www.kevinconner.org for more details about his life and ministry, as well as information about his 75+ books, his video courses, and his audio teaching podcast.

# Kevin's Autobiography

Kevin Conner is known by many people around the world as a theologian, Bible teacher, and best-selling author of over 75 biblical textbooks. Although thousands of people have been impacted by his ministry and his writings, only a few people know his personal story. Kevin took the time to detail his own life journey, including lessons gleaned along the way, in his autobiography "This is My Story" back in 2007. It is now available in the following formats:

- PDF download - visit www.kevinconner.org/shop
- International paperback or eBook from Amazon.
- Australian paperback from WORD books (www.word.com.au).

Kevin was an orphan who never met his dad or mum. He grew up in boy's homes before coming to faith in Jesus Christ in the Salvation Army in his teenage years. From there, his life took many turns as he continued to pursue his faith in God and his understanding of the Scriptures and church life. Follow his journey and gain wisdom for your own life and ministry as you read his intriguing life-story.

# The Foundations of Christian Doctrine

## Video Teaching by Kevin Conner

You can now listen to videos of Kevin Conner's extensive and in-depth teaching on the material contained in his best-selling book 'The Foundation of Christian Doctrine'. There are 67 videos which can be purchased in 4 parts.

Visit www.kevinconner.org/courses for more details.

## About 'The Foundations of Christian Doctrine'

In a decade of church growth and dynamic demonstration of the Holy Spirit's work, God's people still prize the security of a strong Bible foundation. "The Foundations of Christian Doctrine" provides one of the most relevant and clear presentations of the great doctrines of the faith in the years. The text was written to provide an intermediate approach between the more in-depth doctrinal studies and the simplistic. Although originally designed to use in classroom instruction, it lends itself well to study, research and fascinating reading.

## About this Self Study Guide

This Self Study Guide is a companion to the textbook, 'Foundations of Christian Doctrine' by Kevin J. Conner and is designed to be used along with the same. By reading the text and writing the answers, the student will find learning is greatly enriched.

## Acknowledgement

Due credit and very special thanks must go to Ken Malmin (City Bible Church, Portland Oregon, USA) for his work in this Self-Study Guide.

# Endorsements

"Kevin Conner's effort in 'The Foundation of Christian Doctrine' is a landmark work, benefitting usual with a solid view of the theology of rental as it unites with the historic truths of God's Word always embraced by the living church."

**Jack Hayford**, D.Litt.
Former Senior Minister, The Church on the Way Van Nuys, California, USA.

"All over the world I meet ministers who have been impacted and influenced by the books and teaching of Kevin Conner. No one person has changed my world view and had such a profound impact on my life as Kevin. I have given his books to hundreds of ministers around the world. Kevin's grasp of Scripture is astonishing in sound doctrine, rather than chasing all the wild speculations that abound today. Scripture comes alive with Kevin's 'line upon line' teaching styles that lifts the reader to a higher level. Get ready for a high impact, life- changing study that will never leave you the same."

**Rick Godwin**
Senior Minister Eagle's Net Christian Fellowship San Antonio, Texas, USA.

# What Others Say

"We need to move even further away from a purely emotional or experimental base for our Christian lives when discipleship and growth are coming so much on the agenda. This book will prove an invaluable tool for the job …"

"This book lends itself well to study, research and personal reading due to its succinct and readable style …"

"The layout makes it easy to study and read … The book is a must for those who want and need to be more theologically aware …

# Table of Contents

| | |
|---|---|
| Chapter 1 - The Christian Doctrine | 1 |
| Chapter 2 - The Doctrine of Revelation | 5 |
| Chapter 3 - The Doctrine of the Scriptures | 7 |
| Chapter 4 - The Doctrine of God | 11 |
| Chapter 5 - The Doctrine of the Holy Spirit | 17 |
| Chapter 6 - The Doctrine of Angels | 21 |
| Chapter 7 - The Doctrine of Satan and Demonology | 25 |
| Chapter 8 - The Doctrine of Man | 31 |
| Chapter 9 - The Doctrine of Sin | 35 |
| Chapter 10 - The Doctrine of Christ | 39 |
| Chapter 11 - The Doctrine of the Atonement | 45 |
| Chapter 12 - The Doctrine of Eternal States | 57 |
| Other Resources | 61 |

# FOUNDATIONS OF CHRISTIAN DOCTRINE
# SELF- STUDY GUIDE

## Assignment:

The student is to read the assigned chapter and complete the following exercises.

The answers are to be found in careful reading of the textbook. It should be noted that some of the "match appropriate answers" need careful thought as to whether "True" or "False".

Kevin J. Conner

# Chapter 1 – The Christian Doctrine

> It is _____ that Christians be _____ sound Bible _____ and that all doctrine be tested by the _____ _____ of the infallible Word of God. Doctrine _____, _____ and _____ determines a person's _____, _____ and _____.

First fill in the blanks in the above propositional statement. Then answer the following questions.

1. What is "doctrine" and "theology"?

2. Match the following divisions of theology with their particular area of interest (write the number in the underlined area):

    A. _____ Exegetical Theology
    B. _____ Historical Theology
    C. _____ Dogmatic Theology
    D. _____ Biblical Theology
    E. _____ Systematic Theology
    F. _____ Pastoral Theology

    1. The progress of truth through the Bible.
    2. The practical application of theology.
    3. The history of doctrine.
    4. The orderly arrangement of doctrine.
    5. The analysis and interpretation of Scripture.
    6. The formulation of doctrinal creeds.

3. What is the purpose of doctrine?

4. What has caused many churches and Christians to ignore and de-emphasize doctrine?

5. All believers need to know _____ they believe, _____ they believe, and _____ they believe it.

6. What are the three sources of doctrine?

7. What doctrine did Jesus teach?

8. The only sure and infallible test of all doctrine is _____.

9. What are the three symbols of doctrine? What principles do they illustrated?

10. Why must doctrine be obeyed?

11. Which is more important, doctrine or fellowship?

12. How did God reveal doctrine in Scripture? How then should we study the doctrines of Scripture

# Chapter 2 - The Doctrine of Revelation

> The God of the Bible is one who _____ Himself to His creation. God creating man with mental and spiritual faculties indicates His _____ that man _____ Him. However, since the _____ of man, these mental and spiritual faculties have been _____ and he cannot discover God. Thus God, in _____ and _____ has taken by giving a _____ of Himself consummating in the Lord Jesus Christ. Man can only personally know God.

First fill in the blanks in the above propositional statement. Then answer the following questions.

1. What is the theological definition to the word "revelation"?

2. How is man superior to animals?

3. What made man incapable of knowing God on his own?

4. What is the difference between General Revelation and Special Revelation?

5. Define the three General Revelations of God. Also, explain the insufficiency of each one.

6. Match each Special Revelation of God with the phrase that best describes it (write the number in the underlined area):

   A. _____ The revelation of God in Miracles
   B. _____ The Revelation of God in Prophecy
   C. _____ The Revelation of God in Christ
   D. _____ The Revelation of God in Scripture
   E. _____ The Revelation of God in Personal Experience

   1. The ultimate revelation of God
   2. The only infallible revelation we tangibly possess
   3. A revelation of God's infinite knowledge
   4. The purpose of all revelation of God
   5. A revelation of God's power

# Chapter 3 – The Doctrine of the Scriptures

> The Holy _____ are a revelation of God, coming from God and flowing _____ and _____ man. They are the _____ _____ Divine _____ ever given to man and are the _____. _____ in all matters of _____ and _____. The Scriptures were _____-inspired. The Holy Spirit _____ upon the human vessels the very _____ and _____ He wanted written. This word flowed through the _____ channels involving their _____, _____ and _____ _____ _____, without violating such. Yet the Holy Spirit _____ and _____ each _____. _____ and _____ from any error, omission, or inaccuracy.

First fill in the blanks in the above propositional statement. Then answer the following questions.

1. What is the relationship between Jesus and the Bible?

2. Why are the Books of the Bible called "the Oracles of God?"

3. Why are there two Testaments?

4. Match these symbols of the Bible with their meaning (write the number in the underlined area):

   A. _____ Fire
   B. _____ Hammer
   C. _____ Lamp
   D. _____ Mirror
   E. _____ Milk
   F. _____ Seed
   G. _____ Sword
   H. _____ Water
   I. _____ Gold
   J. _____ Bread
   K. _____ Anchor
   L. _____ Meat

   1. Nourishes new Christians
   2. Refreshes and cleanses
   3. Provides safety in storms
   4. Separates the flesh and the spirit
   5. Smashes evil
   6. Priceless value
   7. Cleanses and purges
   8. Strength-giving food
   9. Produces life
   10. Self-revealing
   11. Meant for daily consumption
   12. Gives light in the darkness

5. What is inspiration?

6. What is the difference between revelation, inspiration, and illumination?

7. Explain the problem with each of the six false theories of inspiration.

8. What is plenary-verbal inspiration?

9. Explain how both God and man were involved in the writing of Scripture.

10. What proof do we have that the Bible is really the inspired Word of God?

11. How do the following words apply to the Bible?

    A. Genuineness

    B. Credibility

    C. Canonicity

    D. Infallibility

    E. Authority

12. What is the "Apocrypha"?

# Chapter 4 – The Doctrine of God

> The Scriptures give us the revelation of the eternal _____-_____, who has revealed Himself as _____ _____ existing in _____ _____, even the _____, the _____ and the _____ _____, _____ but _____ in essence; _____, _____, _____ in nature, attributes, power and glory. There is but one eternal Godhead, who is one undivided and indivisible essence; and in this _____ essence there are _____ eternal distinctions, the Father, the Son and the Holy Spirit.

First fill in the blanks in the above propositional statement. Then answer the following questions.

1. Why doesn't the Bible attempt to prove the existence of God?



2. Match the following arguments for the existence of God with the most appropriate phrase from the next page (write the number in the underlined area):

   A. _____ Cosmological Argument
   B. _____ Teleological Argument
   C. _____ Anthropological Argument
   D. _____ Ontological Argument
   E. _____ Moral Argument
   F. _____ Biological Argument
   G. _____ Historical Argument
   H. _____ Christological Argument
   I. _____ Bibliological Argument
   J. _____ Argument From Congruity

1. Life comes only from pre-existent life
2. Intuitive belief in God.
3. Inspiration of Scripture
4. Existence of conscience
5. Harmony of Arguments
6. Design and Purpose
7. Person and work of Christ
8. Cause and Effect
9. Human history
10. Existence of man

3. Briefly define the following non-Christian views of God:

   A. Pantheism

   B. Polytheism

   C. Dualism

   D. Deism

   E. Atheism

   F. Agnosticism

4. What are the four descriptions of God's nature and being?

5. Match the following attributes of God with their definitions (write the number in the underlined area):

   A. _____ Eternal
   B. _____ Self-existent
   C. _____ Immutable
   D. _____ Omnipotent
   E. _____ Omniscient
   F. _____ Omnipresent
   G. _____ Holiness
   H. _____ Righteousness
   I. _____ Love
   J. _____ Faithfulness

   1. The reason of His own existence
   2. Everywhere present
   3. All-powerful
   4. Justice
   5. No beginning or end
   6. Reliable
   7. Unchanging
   8. Self-giving
   9. All knowing
   10. Sinless perfection

6. How can humans know God?

7. When applied to the Godhead, what does the word "Person" mean?

8. What does the word "trinity" mean?

9. What two streams of truth concerning the Godhead must be kept in balance? What will happen if either one is over emphasized?

10. What are the characteristics that distinguish the Father, The Son, and the Holy Spirit from each other?

11. List and explain six natural and Biblical illustrations of the Godhead:

12. Who is the visible part of God?

13. Match the following names of God with their meaning (write the number in the underlined area):

   A. _____ El-Roi
   B. _____ El-Shaddal
   C. _____ El-Olam
   D. _____ El-Gibbor
   E. _____ Elohim-Elyon
   F. _____ Adonai
   G. _____ Jehovah
   H. _____ Jehovah-Jireh
   I. _____ Jehovah-Rapha
   J. _____ Jehovah-Nissi
   K. _____ Jehovah-Mekaddeskum
   L. _____ Jehovah-Shalem
   M. _____ Jehovah-Raah
   N. _____ Jehovah-Tsidkenu
   O. _____ Jehovah-Shammah

   1. I AM THAT I AM
   2. The Lord my Shepherd
   3. The Lord my Banner
   4. Master
   5. The God that Sees
   6. The Lord that Heals
   7. The Everlasting God
   8. The Lord our Peace
   9. The Most High God
   10. The Lord who Sanctifies
   11. The Lord will Provide
   12. The Lord our Righteousness
   13. The Lord is There
   14. The Great God
   15. God Almighty

# Chapter 5 – The Doctrine of the Holy Spirit

> The Holy Spirit is the _____ Divine person of the eternal _____, co-equal, co-eternal, and co-existent with the Father and the Son. It is His ministry to _____ and _____ _____ man as well as to _____ the Son and the Father to the believer. Since the of the Lord Jesus Christ, the Holy Spirit in all His glorious operations is _____ _____ all who believe on the Father through the Son. This is why the present era is known as the _____ _____ _____ _____ _____.

First fill in the blanks in the above propositional statement. Then answer the following questions.

1. Why is it important to study the doctrine of the Holy Spirit?

2. Why is it wrong to view the Holy Spirit as an influence?

3. What proofs do we have that the Holy Spirit is a Person?

    A.

    B.

    C.

    D.

    E.

4. What substantiates the Deity of the Holy Spirit?

5. What was the work of the Holy Spirit in Old Testament times?

   A.

   B.

   C.

   D.

   E.

6. How did the work of the Spirit differ in New Testament times?

7. What is the work of the Holy Spirit as revealed in the New Testament?

   A.

   B.

   C.

   D.

   E.

8. What is the difference between the fruit of the Spirit and the gifts of the Spirit?

9. What is the Holy Spirit's ministry to the unbeliever?

10. Match the following symbols of the Holy Spirit with their significance (write the appropriate number from the list on the next page in the underlined area):
    A. _____ Water
    B. _____ Fire
    C. _____ Wind
    D. _____ Dew
    E. _____ Oil
    F. _____ Dove
    G. _____ Seal
    H. _____ Finger of God
    I. _____ First-fruits
    J. _____ Earnest
    K. _____ Enduement

1. Bringing conviction
2. Refreshing
3. Down payment of full redemption
4. Holiness, purging and zeal
5. Gentleness
6. Clothing for ministry
7. Supernatural enablement
8. Sign of the full harvest
9. Regenerating power
10. Washing, cleansing and fruitfulness
11. Mark of ownership

11. What do the titles of the Holy Spirit illustrate?

# Chapter 6 – The Doctrine of Angels

> The Bible clearly teaches the _____ of angels as mighty _____ _____ beings, whose chief duties are to worship and _____ God. They are not a _____, reproducing themselves, but are a _____ created to minister to heirs of salvation. There are _____ classes of angels, _____ and _____, and man is forbidden to _____ either.

First fill in the blanks in the above propositional statement. Then answer the following questions.

1. What things should we <u>not</u> base our understanding of angels upon? Upon what should this doctrine be built?

2. What is the basic difference between the good and evil angel?

3. Who are the three archangels mentioned in Scripture? What are their different functions?

   A.

   B.

   C.

4. What is the suggested heavenly order of angels?

5. Mark the following statements either true or false:

   A. _____ Angels are eternal.
   B. _____ Angels can assume human form.
   C. _____ Angels are not subject to physical death.
   D. _____ Angels are spoken of as being masculine in gender.
   E. _____ Angels are superior to man.
   F. _____ Being created servants of God, angels really have no will of their own.
   G. _____ All angels worship God.
   H. _____ Angels have no wisdom of their own.
   I. _____ The elect angels have reached a state of sinless perfection.
   J. _____ Angels can speak many languages.
   K. _____ Angels are sons of God.
   L. _____ Some angels have authority over specific nations.
   M. _____ The word "angel" always refers to a spirit being.

5. What are the "Seraphim"?

6. Who are the "Cherubim"?

7. What is the ministry of the elect angels?

8. Why is it that angels do not preach the Gospel?

9. How could the Godhead appear in angelic form?

10. What is a "Theophany"?

11. How does a Theophany differ from the Incarnation?

# Chapter 7 – The Doctrine of Satan and Demonology

> The Scriptures teach the existence of _____ who is the _____ of sin and the _____ over a host of fallen angels and spirits who carry out _____ _____. Christ _____ Satan and the kingdom of _____ at _____ and has commissioned the _____ to deliver men from it and bring them into the kingdom of _____. The _____ _____ of Satan and his forces will be when they are cast into the _____ _____ for eternity.

First fill in the blanks in the above propositional statement. Then answer the following questions.

1. What two extreme views of Satan keep believers out of balance in their understanding?

2. What is the extent of Satan's domain?

3. What was Satan like <u>before</u> his fall?

4. Why did Satan fall?

5. Match the following names and titles of Satan with their meaning (write the number in the underlined area):

   A. _____ Satan
   B. _____ Devil
   C. _____ Serpent
   D. _____ Beelzebub
   E. _____ Lucifer
   F. _____ Belial
   G. _____ Tempter
   H. _____ Accuser
   I. _____ Abaddon
   J. _____ Wicked One

   1. Light-bearer
   2. One charging with an offence
   3. Hurtful, evil one
   4. Worthless, perverse
   5. Adversary, enemy
   6. Destroyer
   7. Enchanter
   8. Enticer
   9. Slanderer
   10. Prince of devils

6. List the seven activities of Satan:

   A.

   B.

   C.

   D.

   E.

   F.

   G.

7. What is the majority of Satan's activity and what is his greatest power?

8. Why does Satan counterfeit God's Kingdom?

9. Why was it that God did not destroy Satan the moment he rebelled?

10. Briefly list the seven steps in Satan's judgment:

   A.

   B.

   C.

   D.

   E.

   F.

   G.

11. What seems to be the difference between fallen angels and demon spirits?

12. List the activities of demons.

13. Can a Christian be "<u>demon-possessed</u>"? Why?

14. What is the Biblical attitude toward the occult?

15. What was the extent of Christ's victory over Satan?

16. "Christ conquered Satan _____, in the three major temptations in the wilderness, and _____, for us, at Calvary in His death, burial, resurrection and ascension."

17. What is the church's ministry in relation to Satan?

18. What must the believer do to be able to resist the devil?

19. How is the soul a spiritual battleground?




20. List the believer's spiritual armour.

# Chapter 8 – The Doctrine of Man

> The Scriptures clearly teach that the original _____ was the direct result of a _____ act of God. Being the masterpiece of creation, man was created in the _____ and _____ of God as a _____ being, consisting of _____, _____ and _____. God created man to have a _____ with Him, to be made into His _____ and likeness, to share in His function of _____ and to be _____ and _____ himself. Though the entrance of _____ seemed to frustrate God's purpose for man in _____ this purpose will be accomplished through _____.

First fill in the blanks in the above propositional statement. Then answer the following questions.

1. What is wrong with the atheistic theory of evolution?

2. What is wrong with theistic evolution?

3. How do we know that man is a created being?

4. Why is man a dependent being?

5. What is meant by the statement that "man is a moral being"?

6. Why was man created with a will?

7. What are the three parts of man? How do they differ from each other?

8. What are the three faculties of the soul?

9. Explain God's four-fold purpose for creating man:

   A.

   B.

   C.

   D.

10. "The purpose of God for man has never changed and will yet be fulfilled through the _____ of Jesus Christ."

# Chapter 9 – The Doctrine of Sin

> Human _____ and man's _____ bear testimony to sin's reality. The Scriptures show that _____ entered the universe through _____ and then into the human race with the _____ of Adam and Eve. The Bible reveals the _____ of sin to be _____-_____ and its tragic result to be _____, but it also reveals God's _____ plan in Christ to make an _____ sin for eternity.

First fill in the blanks in the above propositional statement. Then answer the following questions.

1. Match the following evidences of sin with the most appropriate phrase (write the number in the underlined area):

    A. _____ Creation
    B. _____ Human History
    C. _____ Human Logic
    D. _____ Human Conscience
    E. _____ Human Experience
    F. _____ Human Religions
    G. _____ Believers
    H. _____ Scripture

    1. Discord with man
    2. Heightened awareness of sin
    3. Immorality and crime
    4. Chaos in nature
    5. Wars between nations
    6. Bible declares it
    7. Accusing thoughts
    8. Appeasement of gods

2. Why is a proper concept of sin so important? Explain the chain of reaction.

3. Explain what is wrong with each of the four false theories concerning sin?

    A.

    B.

    C.

    D.

4. What do the cults seek to do by perverting the concept of sin?

5. What is the most Biblical theory concerning how all men have become sinful? How does it differ from the others?

6. List the six Scriptural definitions of sin:

    A.

    B.

    C.

    D.

    E.

    F.

7. Why is "law" necessary?

8. What is the relationship between "sin" and "law"?

9. Where and in whom did sin originate?

10. Why is Satan unredeemable?

11. What is the essence of sin? What is its three-fold progression? "The essence of sin ......

    A.

    B.

    C.

12. What is the meaning of Satan's five "I wills"?

13. How was Adam's temptation different from Lucifer's?

14. How was Satan's temptation aimed at the three parts of man's being?

15. "The serpent's temptations were aimed at …"

16. How did Satan undermine God's Law in tempting Eve?

17. What were the effects of the fall of man?

18. What Divine judgments were pronounced?

19. Explain the "law of sin".

20. What is the highest law?

# Chapter 10 – The Doctrine of Christ

> Scripture reveals that the Lord Jesus Christ is the eternal _____ _____ _____ who _____ existed with the Father and the Holy Spirit, and who by His _____ took upon Himself the form of man and became the _____. In the _____ person of Christ, there are _____ natures, _____ and _____, each in its completeness and integrity. They are _____ but _____, so that He is _____ man and _____ God. It is this _____ _____ of the Divine and human natures which qualifies Him to be the _____ sacrificial _____ between God and man.

First fill in the blanks in the above propositional statement. Then answer the following questions.

1. How may all religions be tested?

2. Match the following heresies concerning the person of Christ with their basic view (write the appropriate number from the list on the next page in the underlined area):

    A. _____ Ebionites
    B. _____ Gnostics
    C. _____ Arians
    D. _____ Apollinarians
    E. _____ Nestorians
    F. _____ Eutychians
    G. _____ Monophysites

1. No human spirit
2. A third nature
3. No divine nature
4. Not two natures
5. No human nature
6. Two persons
7. Created being

3. What is the Orthodox position concerning the person of Christ?

4. What problem was there in understanding the Old Testament prophecies concerning the person of Christ?

5. Why is belief in the virgin birth so important?

6. What does "incarnation" mean?

7. What proof do we have of the virgin birth?

8. Why was it that no descendant of Adam could redeem man?

9. Why did God have to become a man to redeem man?

10. What is true and what is not true about Christ's "self-emptying"?

11. List the nine reasons for the incarnation:

    A.

    B.

    C.

    D.

    E.

    F.

    G.

    H.

    I.

12. Are the following statements either true or false?

    A. _____ Christ being called the Son of God means that He was "begotten" in the incarnation.
    B. _____ Jesus existed before He was born of the Virgin Mary.
    C. _____ Jesus is self-existent.
    D. _____ Jesus is limited in power now.
    E. _____ Jesus is present only in heaven right now.
    F. _____ Jesus is immutable.
    G. _____ Jesus to called the "everlasting Father" in the Scripture but this does not make Him to be THE Father.
    H. _____ Jesus is the "I AM".
    I. _____ Scripturally speaking, we should not pray to Jesus but should pray to the Father in the Name of the Son.
    J. _____ Jesus is called "the Angel of Jehovah".
    K. _____ In His "self-emptying" Jesus did not claim to be equal with God.
    L. _____ JESUS is the Name of the Son's humanity.
    M. _____ The body of Jesus was different from our body physically.
    N. _____ Jesus had to "learn obedience".
    O. _____ Jesus was limited in His human knowledge.
    P. _____ Jesus still has a human body with sinless infirmities, but now glorified.

13. Why was it necessary that Christ be sinless?

14. What is sinlessness?

15. Explain the three theories concerning the sinlessness of Christ.

16. How was Jesus' and Adam's temptations different from ours? How was Jesus' different from Adam's?

17. What kind of temptation did Jesus not suffer?

18. What carried Jesus' human nature through the temptations victoriously?

19. Why didn't Jesus have to die?

20. How is Christ our example?

21. What is a "mediator"? How does Christ fulfil this role?

22. How are the two natures, human and divine, united with Christ?

23. What qualifies Jesus to be the only mediator between God and man?

# Chapter 11 – The Doctrine of the Atonement

> The Doctrine of the Atonement comprises the _____ work of Christ, involving His _____, _____, _____, _____, _____, _____, _____ and _____ _____.
>
> The plan of the atonement _____ in the counsels of the eternal Godhead _____ the creation and fall of man. It is being accomplished in _____ through the work of Christ and the _____ of it that are realized by man on _____ terms will continue for _____. Such a _____ is a revelation of the _____ _____ of the Almighty God.

First fill in the blanks in the above propositional statement. Then answer the following questions.

1. What work did Christ come to do?

2. Why was the atonement necessary?

3. What is God's wrath?

4. What is the atonement?

5. How does the atonement solve the dilemma between God's wrath and God's love?

6. When was the atonement first planned?

7. List the nine things most all religions of nations believe in:

   A.

   B.

   C.

   D.

   E.

   F.

   G.

   H.

   I.

8.  How did Israel differ from other nations in those basic areas of belief?

9.  How is Christ's death unique?

10. Match the following false views of the death of Christ with the most appropriate phrase (write the number in the underlined area):

    A. _____ Accident Theory
    B. _____ Martyr Theory
    C. _____ Moral Influence Theory
    D. _____ Governmental Theory
    E. _____ Commercial Theory
    F. _____ Eradication Theory

    1. An example of hatred for sin
    2. Purified Adam's sinful nature
    3. Died for a good cause
    4. A payment to Satan
    5. Unfortunate tragedy
    6. Suffering for others

11. Write a brief paragraph summarizing the Scriptural view of Christ's death.

12. Define the three kinds of death. How did Christ taste each one?

    A.

    B.

    C.

13. Where was Jesus during the three days and nights after His death on the cross?

14. Why was the resurrection of Christ necessary?

15. What are some of the proofs of the resurrection? List at least four.

    A.

    B.

    C.

    D.

16. What is the ascension of Christ foundational for? How does it differ from the translation of other men?

17. What is the significance of Christ's glorification?




18. What are the two major aspects of Christ's exaltation?

    A.

    B.

19. What does the word "session" mean in relation to Christ's ministry? How long will it last?




20. How much is the second coming of Christ emphasized in Scripture? Why?




21. What is the practical value of the doctrine of Christ's second coming?

22. What are the two kinds of judgment presently?

    A.

    B.

23. Who will Christ judge in the future?

24. What is "grace"?

25. "Grace is not _____ coming to _____ but _____ coming to _____."

26. What is "redemption"?

27. How did Christ fulfil the role of the Kinsman Redeemer?

28. How is "ransom" different from "redemption"? What is the price that Christ paid?

29. What is meant by the statement that "Christ's death was substitutionary"?

30. What does "propitiation" mean? How was it fulfilled in Christ?

31. What is "reconciliation"? How does it apply to the work of Christ?

32. How is the atonement both necessary and possible?

33. How did Christ fulfil the Day of Atonement ceremonies?

34. "The atonement is the actual and official _____."

35. Why is it that everyone will not be saved?

36. How does Thiessen define "election"?

37. How does "election of eternity" differ from "election of time"?

38. What Is "foreknowledge"? How does it relate to election?

39. What is "predestination"? How does it relate to election and foreknowledge?

40. How does Thiessen define "calling"?

41. "God in His grace, on the basis of _____."

42. What is the first word of the Gospel?

43. What are some false concepts of repentance?




44. What is repentance? What are its three elements?

    A.

    B.

    C.

45. What are the fruits of repentance? List at least four.

    A.

    B.

    C.

    D.

46. What Is the second word of the Gospel? How does it differ from repentance?




47. What are some false concepts of faith?




48. What is faith? What is its source?

49. What are the five kinds of faith?

   A.

   B.

   C.

   D.

   E.

50. What is the theological definition of "assurance"?

51. What are the means of assurance?

52. What are the two streams of truth concerning the security of the believer?

53. What is the difference between backsliding and apostasy?

54. What is the security of the believer conditional upon?

55. What are the two means of grace? Why are they so important?

   A.

   B.

56. What does "justification" mean? How can man be justified?

57. What three things are involved in justification?

58. Regeneration "is the Divine act by which _____."

59. What is "adoption"? How does it relate to regeneration?

60. What are the five elements of "sanctification"?

   A.

   B.

   C.

   D.

   E.

61. How does the Biblical view of sanctification differ from the false views?

62. What are the means of sanctification?

63. What are the three kinds of "perfection"? How do they differ from each other?

64. "Thus the believer is exhorted to _____."

65. How will the saints be "glorified"?

66. How does salvation relate to time?

# Chapter 12 – Doctrine of Eternal States

> The Scriptures teach that man is on _____ during his time on earth. Those who _____ to God's _____ and _____ Him will be eternally rewarded in _____, God's dwelling place. Those who willfully _____ the grace of God, do their _____ _____ and serve Satan will be eternally punished in _____, Satan's dwelling place. Eternal destinies are settled here in _____.

First fill in the blanks in the above propositional statement. Then answer the following questions.

1. What does "Time" represent to man? What does "Eternity" represent?

2. How has God shown us in time what He will do in eternity?

3. Briefly define the various arrangements God has made with man during time.

4. How is "resurrection" linked with "judgment"?

5. What are the two resurrections?

6. What will the coming day of judgment be like?

7. How will believers be judged?

8. Why is it necessary that unbelievers be judged?

9. Define the three heavens:

   A.

   B.

   C.

10. Define the three divisions of hell:

    A.

    B.

    C.

11. What is Gehenna? What will it be like?

# Other Resources
## Other Books by Kevin Conner

- Acts, A Commentary
- An Evaluation of Joseph Prince's Book 'Destined to Reign'
- Are Women Elders Biblical?
- Biblical Principles of Leadership
- The Christian Millennium
- 1 & 2 Chronicles, a Commentary
- 1 Corinthians, a Commentary
- The Church in the New Testament
- The Church of the Firstborn and the Birthright
- 1 & 2 Chronicles, A Commentary
- The Covenants (with Ken Malmin)
- Daily Devotions (or Ministrations)
- Daniel, An Exposition
- The Day After the Sabbath
- The Death-Resurrection Route
- Deuteronomy, A Commentary
- Esther, A Commentary
- Eternity, Where Will You Spend It?
- Exodus, A Commentary
- Ezekiel, A Commentary
- The Feasts of Israel
- First Principles of the Doctrine of Christ
- Foundations of Christian Doctrine
- Foundations of Christian Doctrine (Self Study Guide)
- Foundational Principles of Church Membership
- Foundation Principles of the Doctrine of Christ
- Frequently Asked Questions
- Galatians, A Commentary
- Genesis, A Commentary
- Headship, Covering and Hats
- Hebrews, A Commentary
- The House of God
- Interpreting the Book of Revelation
- Interpreting the Scriptures (with Ken Malmin)
- Interpreting the Scriptures (Self Study Guide)

- Interpreting the Symbols and Types
- Isaiah, A Commentary
- James, A Commentary
- Jeremiah and Lamentations, A Commentary
- Joshua, A Commentary
- Jude, A Commentary
- Judges, A Commentary
- Keep Yourself Pure
- The Kingdom Cult of Self
- Kings of the Kingdom - Character Studies on Israel's Kings
- Law and Grace
- Leviticus, A Commentary
- The Lord Jesus Christ our Melchizedek Priest
- Maintaining the Presence
- Marriage, Divorce and Remarriage
- Messages from Matthew
- Methods and Principles of Bible Research
- Ministries in the Cluster
- The Ministry of Women
- The Minor Prophets, A Commentary Mystery
- Mystery Parables of the Kingdom
- The Name of God
- New Covenant Realities
- New Testament Survey (with Ken Malmin)
- Numbers, A Commentary
- Old Testament Survey (with Ken Malmin)
- Only for Catholics
- Passion Week Chart
- Philippians, A Commentary
- Psalms, A Commentary
- The Relevance of the Old Testament to a New Testament Church Restoration Theology
- Restoration Theology
- Revelation, A Commentary
- Romans, A Commentary
- The Royal Seed
- Ruth, A Commentary
- 1 & 2 Samuel, A Commentary

- Sermon Outlines (4 volumes)
- The Seventy Weeks Prophecy
- Studies in the Royal Priesthood
- The Sword and Consequences
- The Tabernacle of David
- The Tabernacle of Moses
- The Temple of Solomon
- Table Talks
- Tale of Three Trees
- 1 & 2 Thessalonians, A Commentary
- This is My Story (Kevin Conner's autobiography)
- This We Believe
- Three Days and Three Nights (with Chart)
- Tithes and Offerings
- Today's Prophets
- To Drink or Not to Drink
- To Smoke or Not to Smoke
- Two Kings and a Prince
- Understanding the New Birth and the Baptism of the Holy Spirit
- Vision of an Antioch Church
- Water Baptism Thesis
- What About Israel?

Visit www.kevinconner.org for more information.
Visit www.amazon.com/author/kevinjconner for a list of other books by Kevin Conner

## Video Training Seminars

Kevin Conner's popular "Key of Knowledge" Seminar is now available as an online teaching course. Part 1 covers 'Methods and Principles of Bible Research' and includes over 6 hours of video teaching, the required textbooks, extra hand out notes, and a self-guided online study program. The first lesson, 'Challenge to Study' is FREE.

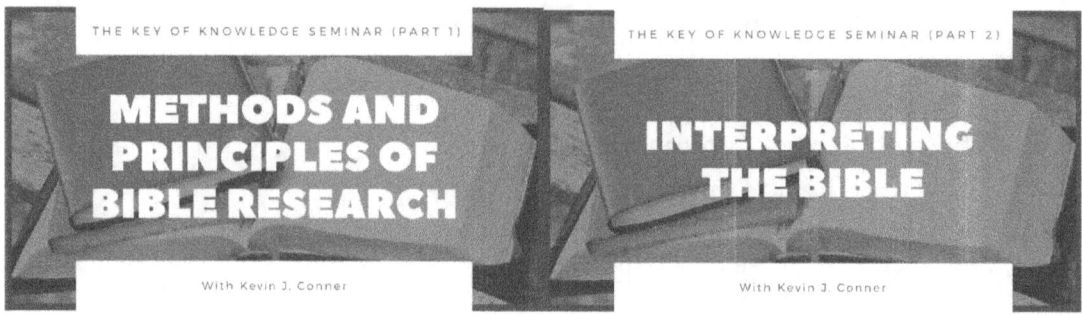

The second part of Kevin Conner's "Key of Knowledge" Seminar is about 'Interpreting the Bible' and includes over 7 hours of video teaching, two downloadable textbooks, extra hand out notes, and a self-guided online study program. These two courses can be taken as stand-alone courses, in succession, or simultaneously.

Also available at www.kevinconner.org/courses is Kevin's extensive teaching on his best-selling book The Foundation of Christian Doctrine, which includes 67 videos which can be purchased in 4 parts.

Visit the courses page at www.kevinconner.org for all the details.

## Kevin Conner's Audio Teaching

Dozens of Kevin Conner's messages are available on his FREE teaching podcast - 'Kevin Conner Teaches'. This podcast is accessible from Apple Podcasts, Google Podcasts, or Spotify Podcasts (if you are a subscriber), as well as at www.kevinconner.podbean.com (including on the Podbean mobile App).

New messages are published weekly, selected from messages Kevin has given over the years at various churches, conferences, and training seminars. Be sure to subscribe so you are notified of recent releases.

Visit https://www.kevinconner.org/audios-by-kevin/ for a full list of podcast titles and series.

## PDF Versions of Kevin Conner's Books

All of Kevin Conner's books are now available to purchase in quality PDF format. This digital format is in addition to the Kindle eBooks and paperback/hardback versions currently available. A PDF is a 'portable document format' used on all computers for reading documents. Books in this format can be read on a computer, laptop, or handheld device and/or printed out for your personal use (even stored in your own binding of choice). Many PDF readers also allow you to 'mark-up' and add your own notes to the document. PDFs of Kevin's books are for your personal use and are not for copying or redistribution.

You can purchase PDF books at www.kevinconner.org/shop. Upon payment, a download link will be sent to you via email along with your receipt.

# Resources by Mark Conner

Kevin Conner's son, Mark Conner, worked closely with him in the church ministry for many years (as music director and youth pastor), before succeeding him in 1995 as the Senior Minister of what was then Waverley Christian Fellowship (now CityLife Church) Mark transitioned out of that role in early 2017 and since that time has been giving himself to speaking, training, coaching, and writing.

Here is a list of Mark's books which may be of interest to you:
- Transforming Your Church - Seven Strategic Shifts
- Money Talks: Practical Wisdom for Becoming Financially Free
- The Spiritual Journey: Understanding the Stages of Faith
- How to Avoid Burnout: Five Habits of Healthy Living
- Prison Break: Finding Personal Freedom
- Pass the Baton: Successful Leadership Transition
- Successful Christian Ministry

These can be purchased from:
- Amazon.com/author/markconner in paperback and eBook format.
- WORD books in Australia (www.word.com.au)
- www.kevinconner.org/books-by-mark-conner in PDF format.

Mark also has an active BLOG and teaching podcast. Visit www.markconner.com.au for more information.

www.ingramcontent.com/pod-product-compliance
Lightning Source LLC
Chambersburg PA
CBHW082246300426
44110CB00039B/2453